BUILDING GENERA

A DEEP DIVE INTO LLM ARCHITECTURE AND TRAINING

OLIVER LUCAS JR

Copyright © 2024 by Oliver Lucas Jr

All rights reserved. No part of this publication may be reproduced, distributed, or transmitted in any form or by any means, including photocopying, recording, or other electronic or mechanical methods, without the prior written permission of the publisher, except in the case of brief quotations embodied in critical reviews and certain other non commercial uses permitted by copyright law.

TABLE OF CONTENTS

Chapter 4

Chapter 5

Chapter 6

Chapter 7

Chapter 8

Chapter 9

Chapter 10

Preface

The world is abuzz with the transformative potential of Artificial Intelligence, and at the forefront of this revolution are Large Language Models (LLMs). These incredible feats of engineering are not just reshaping how we interact with technology, but they're also redefining what's possible in fields ranging from creative writing and code development to scientific research and beyond.

This book, "Building Generative AI: A Deep Dive into LLM Architecture and Training," is your guide to understanding and mastering the intricacies of LLMs. Whether you're a seasoned AI researcher, a curious developer, or simply someone intrigued by the possibilities of this technology, this book will equip you with the knowledge and skills to navigate the exciting world of LLMs.

We'll embark on a journey that starts with the foundational concepts of Natural Language Processing and culminates in the deployment and scaling of real-world LLM applications. Along the way, we'll delve into the groundbreaking Transformer architecture, explore the art of prompt engineering, and grapple with the ethical considerations that come with building powerful AI systems.

This book is more than just a technical manual; it's an exploration of the creative potential and societal impact of LLMs. We'll examine how these models are being used to generate stunning works of art, write code with unprecedented efficiency, and even push the boundaries of scientific discovery.

But we won't shy away from the challenges and responsibilities that come with this technology. We'll delve into the critical issues of bias, misinformation, and ethical AI development, providing you with the tools and knowledge to build and deploy LLMs responsibly.

By the end of this book, you'll not only understand the inner workings of LLMs but also be equipped to build your own, fine-tune them for specific tasks, and deploy them in real-world applications. More importantly, you'll gain a deeper understanding of the transformative power of generative AI and its potential to reshape our world.

So, join me on this exciting journey into the heart of LLMs. Let's explore the fascinating world of generative AI together and unlock the incredible possibilities that lie ahead.

Chapter 1

Introduction to Generative AI and LLMs

1.1 Introduction: What is Generative AI?

Imagine a world where artificial intelligence can compose breathtaking symphonies, paint masterpieces that rival human artists, and write compelling stories that capture the imagination. This is not a scene from a science fiction movie; it's the reality of generative AI, a revolutionary technology that is transforming the way we interact with machines and pushing the boundaries of creative expression.

Generative AI, at its core, is a branch of artificial intelligence that focuses on creating new content, whether it's text, images, music, code, or even 3D models. Unlike traditional AI systems that analyze and interpret existing data, generative AI goes a step further by generating entirely novel outputs. It's like having an AI partner that can not only understand your requests but also bring your ideas to life in ways you never thought possible.

The key to this creative power lies in the ability of generative AI to learn patterns and structures from vast amounts of data. By analyzing millions of examples, these systems can identify underlying relationships and generate new content that adheres to those learned patterns. This allows them to produce outputs that are not merely copies of existing data but rather unique creations that exhibit originality and ingenuity.

One of the early breakthroughs in generative AI was the invention of Generative Adversarial Networks (GANs). These networks consist of two components: a generator that creates new content and a discriminator that evaluates the quality of the generated output. Through a process of competition and collaboration, these two components push each other to improve, resulting in increasingly realistic and sophisticated creations.

Another major milestone was the development of the Transformer architecture, a neural network design that has revolutionized natural language processing. Transformers excel at capturing long-range dependencies in text, enabling them to generate coherent and contextually relevant language. This breakthrough has paved the way for the creation of large language models (LLMs) that can understand and generate human-like text with remarkable fluency.

From chatbots that engage in natural conversations to AI assistants that write code and compose music, generative AI is already having a profound impact on various industries. As we delve deeper into this book, we will explore the fascinating world of generative AI, uncovering its underlying mechanisms, its vast potential, and the transformative power it holds for the future.

1.2 Understanding Large Language Models: Core Concepts and Capabilities

Now that we've established a foundation for generative AI, let's dive deeper into the heart of this technology: Large Language Models (LLMs). These powerful engines drive many of the most impressive generative AI applications we see today. But what exactly are they, and what makes them so special?

At their core, LLMs are a type of artificial intelligence that has been trained on a massive amount of text data. This data could include books, articles, code, websites, and even social media posts. By processing this vast sea of information, LLMs learn to identify patterns, understand grammar and syntax, and even grasp the nuances of human language.

Think of an LLM as a super-powered language student who has devoured every book in the library and absorbed the knowledge of countless conversations. This deep learning process allows LLMs to:

Understand and interpret human language: They can analyze text, identify key concepts, and extract meaning from complex sentences.

Generate human-like text: They can produce coherent and grammatically correct text, ranging from short answers to long-form articles.

Translate between languages: They can accurately translate text from one language to another, bridging communication gaps.

Summarize information: They can condense lengthy documents into concise summaries, saving time and effort.

Answer questions: They can provide informative and relevant answers to a wide range of questions, acting as a knowledgeable resource.

Engage in conversations: They can participate in natural and engaging conversations, responding to prompts and queries in a human-like manner.

But what sets LLMs apart from traditional language models? The answer lies in their sheer size and complexity. LLMs are built on deep neural networks with billions, or even trillions, of parameters. These parameters are like the connections between neurons in the human brain, allowing the model to learn and represent complex relationships between words and concepts.

The more parameters an LLM has, the more nuanced its understanding of language becomes. This allows it to generate more coherent, contextually relevant, and creative text. It's like comparing a small dictionary to a vast encyclopedia – the larger the knowledge base, the richer the understanding.

Furthermore, LLMs leverage a revolutionary architecture called the Transformer. This architecture, based on the concept of "attention," allows the model to focus on the most relevant parts of the input when generating output. This enables LLMs to capture long-range dependencies in text and understand the relationships between words even when they are far apart in a sentence.

In essence, LLMs are not just sophisticated pattern-matching machines; they are powerful engines of language understanding and generation. They represent a significant leap forward in artificial intelligence, opening up a world of possibilities for how we interact with machines and create new forms of content.

1.3 Applications and Impact of Generative AI

The rise of generative AI, and LLMs in particular, is not just a technological marvel; it's a cultural and economic shift with the potential to reshape how we live, work, and interact with the world around us. Let's explore some of the most impactful applications of this technology:

1. Revolutionizing Communication: The Rise of AI Chatbots

Imagine customer service that's available 24/7, instantly responds to your queries, and can even anticipate your needs.[1] This is the power of LLMs in chatbots. They can engage in natural, human-like conversations, providing information, answering questions, and even offering emotional support.[2] Beyond customer service, LLM-powered chatbots are transforming education (as AI tutors), healthcare (as virtual assistants for patients), and even entertainment (as interactive characters in games and virtual worlds).[3]

2. Unleashing Creativity: Content Creation and Beyond

Generative AI is a game-changer for creative industries.[4] LLMs can write compelling marketing copy, generate scripts for films and videos, compose music in various styles, and even assist in writing novels or poetry.[5] This doesn't replace human creativity, but it provides powerful tools for artists, writers, and musicians to explore new ideas and enhance their work.[6]

3. Accelerating Productivity: Code Generation and Software Development

LLMs are transforming the way software is built.[7] They can generate code in multiple programming languages, assist with debugging, and even create entire applications from natural language descriptions.[8] This not only speeds up development but also allows people with limited coding experience to bring their software ideas to life.[9]

4. Breaking Barriers: Language Translation and Accessibility

LLMs are making the world a more connected place through advanced language translation.[10] They can translate text with greater accuracy and nuance than ever before, facilitating cross-cultural communication and understanding.[11] Additionally, LLMs can help create tools for people with disabilities, such as generating image captions for the visually impaired or converting speech to text for those with hearing impairments.[12]

5. Beyond Text: Multimodal AI and the Future

While we've focused on text-based applications, generative AI is rapidly expanding into other domains.[13] Multimodal LLMs can process and generate images, audio, and even video, opening up exciting possibilities in fields like:[14]

Drug discovery: Generating new drug candidates and predicting their effectiveness.[15]

Materials science: Designing new materials with specific properties.[16]

Personalized education: Creating customized learning experiences tailored to individual needs.[17]

The Impact on Society

The widespread adoption of LLMs will undoubtedly have a profound impact on society. While there are concerns about job displacement and the potential for misuse, there are also immense opportunities for increased productivity, creativity, and accessibility.[18] As we move forward, it's crucial to develop these technologies responsibly, ensuring fairness, transparency, and ethical use.

Chapter 2

Foundations of Natural Language Processing

2.1 Text Preprocessing and Representation: Tokenization, Embeddings, and More

Before we can unleash the power of LLMs, we need to equip them with the ability to understand human language. This is where Natural Language Processing (NLP) comes into play. NLP is a field of artificial intelligence that focuses on enabling computers to understand, interpret, and manipulate human language.[1] And at the heart of NLP lies the crucial step of **text preprocessing**.

Think of text preprocessing as preparing a delicious meal. Before you can cook, you need to gather your ingredients, clean them, and chop them into manageable pieces. Similarly, before an LLM can process text, we need to transform raw text data into a format that it can understand and learn from.

Tokenization: Breaking Down the Text

The first step in this process is **tokenization**. Imagine a sentence like "The quick brown fox jumps over the lazy dog." To a computer, this is just a string of characters. Tokenization breaks this string down into individual units, or **tokens**, such as "The", "quick", "brown", "fox", etc. These tokens become the building blocks for further analysis.

There are different approaches to tokenization:

Word-level tokenization: This is the most straightforward approach, where each word becomes a token.

Character-level tokenization: Here, each individual character becomes a token.

Subword tokenization: This approach breaks words down into smaller units, allowing the model to handle rare or unseen words more effectively.

The choice of tokenization method depends on the specific task and the nature of the language being processed.

Embeddings: Representing Words in a Numerical Space

Once we have our tokens, we need to represent them in a way that captures their meaning and relationships. This is where **embeddings** come in. Embeddings are dense vector representations of words, where each word is mapped to a point in a high-dimensional space.

The beauty of embeddings is that they capture semantic relationships between words. Words with similar meanings are closer together in this space, while words with different meanings are farther apart. This allows LLMs to understand that "king" and "queen" are related concepts, while "cat" and "car" are not.

There are various techniques for creating embeddings, including:

Word2Vec: This popular method learns embeddings by predicting the context of a word within a sentence.

GloVe: This method learns embeddings by analyzing the co-occurrence of words in a large corpus of text.

FastText: This method extends Word2Vec by considering subword information, improving the representation of rare words.

Beyond Tokenization and Embeddings

Text preprocessing involves several other important steps, such as:

Stop word removal: Removing common words like "the", "a", and "is" that carry little semantic meaning.

Stemming and lemmatization: Reducing words to their base forms to improve consistency.

Lowercasing: Converting all text to lowercase to avoid treating the same word differently due to capitalization.

By carefully preprocessing text, we transform raw data into a structured and meaningful representation that LLMs can effectively learn from. This lays the foundation for the impressive capabilities of these models to understand, generate, and manipulate human language.

2.2 Language Modeling: Statistical and Neural Approaches

Now that we've learned how to prepare text data for processing, let's explore the core concept of **language modeling**. Essentially, language modeling is the task of teaching a computer to understand the probabilities and relationships between words in a language. This allows the computer to predict the next word in a sequence, judge the grammatical correctness of a sentence, and even generate new text that sounds natural.

Historically, there have been two main approaches to language modeling: statistical and neural.

Statistical Language Models: Counting and Predicting

Statistical language models rely on statistical analysis of large text corpora to learn the probabilities of word sequences. One of the most common techniques is the **n-gram model**. An n-gram is a sequence of 'n' words. For example:

Unigram: Single words (e.g., "the", "cat", "sat")

Bigram: Two-word sequences (e.g., "the cat", "cat sat", "sat on")

Trigram: Three-word sequences (e.g., "the cat sat", "cat sat on", "sat on the")

These models calculate the probability of a word given its preceding words. For instance, a trigram model might learn that the probability of the word "mat" following the sequence "the cat sat on the" is quite high.

While simple and efficient, statistical language models have limitations:

Sparsity: They struggle with rare or unseen word combinations, as they rely on observing those combinations in the training data.

Limited context: They can only consider a limited context window (e.g., the previous two words in a trigram model).

Neural Language Models: Learning Complex Relationships

Neural language models, on the other hand, leverage the power of neural networks to learn more complex and nuanced relationships between words. These models use **word embeddings** (which we discussed in the previous section) to represent words as vectors in a high-dimensional space.

Recurrent Neural Networks (RNNs) were early pioneers in neural language modeling. RNNs have a "memory" that allows them to process sequences of words while considering the context of previous words. However, RNNs can struggle to capture long-range dependencies in text.

This is where **Transformers** come in. As we'll explore in the next chapter, Transformers excel at capturing long-range dependencies thanks to their attention mechanism. This allows them to learn more sophisticated language patterns and generate more coherent and contextually relevant text.

The Benefits of Neural Language Models

Neural language models offer several advantages over statistical approaches:

Better handling of sparsity: They can generalize to unseen word combinations more effectively.

Wider context window: They can consider a much larger context when predicting words.

Improved performance: They generally achieve higher accuracy in language modeling tasks.

The evolution from statistical to neural language models has been a significant leap forward in NLP. Neural models, particularly those based on Transformers, have paved the way for the development of powerful LLMs that are transforming the field of AI.

2.3 Sequence-to-Sequence Models: The Building Blocks of LLMs

Imagine you're translating a sentence from English to Spanish. You're not just substituting words; you're understanding the meaning of the entire sentence and then reconstructing it in a different language. This process of mapping one sequence (the English sentence) to another sequence (the Spanish translation) is the essence of **sequence-to-sequence (seq2seq) models**.

Seq2seq models are a powerful type of neural network architecture that has become a fundamental building block for many LLMs. They are designed to handle tasks where both the input and output are sequences of variable length.

The Encoder-Decoder Structure

A seq2seq model typically consists of two main components:

Encoder: This part of the network processes the input sequence (e.g., the English sentence) and compresses its information into a fixed-length vector called the **context vector** or **hidden state**. Think of this as capturing the essence of the input sequence.

Decoder: This part takes the context vector and generates the output sequence (e.g., the Spanish translation) one element at a time. It uses the information encoded in the context vector and the previously generated elements to predict the next element in the sequence.

How Seq2Seq Models Work

Let's break down the process with our translation example:

1 Encoding: The encoder reads the English sentence ("The cat sat on the mat") word by word. Each word is converted into an embedding, and the encoder processes these embeddings sequentially, updating its internal state with each word. The final state of the encoder becomes the context vector, which represents the meaning of the entire sentence.

2 Decoding: The decoder starts with a special "start" token and uses the context vector to predict the first word in the Spanish translation ("El").

3 Generating the Sequence: The decoder then takes the generated word ("El") and the context vector to predict the next word ("gato"). This process continues, with the decoder using the previously generated words and the context vector to predict the next word in the sequence, until it generates a special "end" token, signaling the completion of the translation.

Applications of Seq2Seq Models

Seq2seq models have a wide range of applications beyond machine translation, including:

Text summarization: Condensing long articles into shorter summaries.

Question answering: Generating answers to questions based on given text.

Dialogue generation: Creating chatbots that can engage in conversations.

Speech recognition: Converting spoken language into text.

Image captioning: Generating descriptions of images.

Seq2Seq Models and LLMs

While many modern LLMs rely primarily on the Transformer architecture, seq2seq models remain an important foundation. They introduced the concept of encoding and decoding sequences, which is crucial for tasks like machine translation and text summarization. Furthermore, understanding seq2seq models provides a valuable stepping stone to understanding more complex architectures like Transformers, which we'll explore in the next chapter.

Chapter 3

The Transformer Architecture

3.1 Attention is All You Need: The Breakthrough of Transformers

The year 2017 marked a turning point in the world of Natural Language Processing (NLP) with the publication of a groundbreaking research paper titled "Attention is All You Need." This paper introduced the **Transformer**, a novel neural network architecture that has since revolutionized the field and become the foundation for many state-of-the-art LLMs.

Before Transformers, Recurrent Neural Networks (RNNs) were the dominant architecture for NLP tasks. While RNNs were effective in processing sequential data, they had limitations, particularly when dealing with long sequences. They processed information step-by-step, which could be slow and inefficient, and they struggled to capture long-range dependencies in text.

Transformers addressed these limitations by abandoning the sequential processing of RNNs and introducing a mechanism called **attention**. This mechanism allows the model to focus on the most relevant parts of the input when processing information, regardless of their position in the sequence.

The Power of Attention

Imagine you're reading a sentence: "The cat, which was sitting on the mat, purred softly." To understand the meaning of "purred," you need to connect it to "cat," even though they are several words apart. Attention allows Transformers to do precisely this – to weigh the importance of different words in the input when processing a specific word.

In the context of Transformers, attention can be thought of as a mechanism for dynamically assigning weights to different parts of the input sequence. These weights determine how much "attention" the model should pay to each word when processing another word.

How Attention Works in Transformers

The attention mechanism in Transformers involves three main steps:

1 Calculating attention scores: For each word in the input sequence, the model calculates attention scores with respect to all other words. These scores indicate how much each word should be "attended to" when processing the current word.

2 Normalizing attention scores: The attention scores are normalized using a softmax function, ensuring they sum up to 1. This creates a probability distribution over the input words.

3 Weighted sum: The model creates a weighted sum of the values of all input words, where the weights are the normalized attention scores. This weighted sum represents the context for the current word, taking into account the relevance of other words in the sequence.

Benefits of Transformers

The introduction of attention and the Transformer architecture brought several key advantages:

Parallelization: Unlike RNNs, Transformers can process the entire input sequence in parallel, leading to significant speed improvements during training.

Long-range dependencies: Attention allows Transformers to capture relationships between words that are far apart in the sequence, improving performance on tasks that require understanding long-range context.

Improved performance: Transformers have achieved state-of-the-art results on a wide range of NLP tasks, including machine translation, text summarization, and[1] question answering.

The "Attention is All You Need" paper marked a paradigm shift in NLP. Transformers have become the dominant architecture for LLMs, enabling the development of powerful models like BERT, GPT, and LaMDA, which are transforming the way we interact with machines and understand human language.

3.2 Encoder-Decoder Structure: Understanding the Flow of Information

While the attention mechanism is a core component of Transformers, it's important to understand how this mechanism fits into the overall architecture. Like the seq2seq models we discussed earlier, Transformers also utilize an **encoder-decoder structure**. However, the way information flows and is processed within this structure differs significantly.

The Encoder: Processing the Input

The encoder in a Transformer is responsible for taking the input sequence (e.g., a sentence) and transforming it into a rich, contextualized representation. This is achieved through a stack of identical layers, each performing two main functions:

1 **Self-Attention:** This is where the magic happens. The self-attention mechanism allows each word in the input sequence to "attend" to all other words in the sequence, capturing relationships and dependencies between them. This creates a

representation of each word that takes into account its context within the entire sequence.

2 Feed-Forward Neural Network: After self-attention, each word's representation is passed through a feed-forward neural network. This network applies a non-linear transformation to the representation, further refining it and capturing more complex patterns.

This process is repeated for each layer in the encoder stack, with each layer building upon the representations created by the previous layer. The output of the final encoder layer is a sequence of vectors, where each vector represents a word in the input sequence, enriched with contextual information.

The Decoder: Generating the Output

The decoder in a Transformer takes the encoded representation of the input and generates the output sequence (e.g., a translated sentence, a summary, or an answer to a question). It also consists of a stack of identical layers, each performing three main functions:

1 Masked Self-Attention: Similar to the encoder, the decoder uses self-attention to allow each word in the output sequence to attend to all preceding words in the output sequence. The "masked" part is crucial: it prevents the decoder from "looking ahead" at future words in the output sequence, ensuring that the generation process remains sequential.

2 Encoder-Decoder Attention: This is where the decoder interacts with the encoder's output. The decoder attends to the encoded representations of the input sequence, allowing it to utilize the information captured by the encoder.

3 Feed-Forward Neural Network: Similar to the encoder, the decoder also employs a feed-forward neural network to further refine the representations.

The decoder generates the output sequence one element at a time. It starts with a special "start" token and uses the encoded input and the previously generated words to predict the next word in the sequence. This process continues until a special "end" token is generated, signaling the completion of the output.

The Flow of Information

In essence, information flows through a Transformer as follows:

The input sequence is fed into the encoder.

The encoder processes the input using self-attention and feed-forward networks, creating a contextualized representation.

The decoder takes the encoded representation and generates the output sequence step-by-step, using masked self-attention, encoder-decoder attention, and feed-forward networks.

This encoder-decoder structure, combined with the powerful attention mechanism, allows Transformers to effectively capture relationships between words, process information in parallel, and generate high-quality outputs for a wide range of NLP tasks.

3.3 Self-Attention Mechanisms: Capturing Contextual Relationships

We've mentioned "attention" several times now, but let's delve deeper into the heart of Transformers: the **self-attention mechanism**. This is where the true magic happens, allowing these models to capture intricate relationships between words in a sentence, regardless of their distance from each other.

Understanding Self-Attention

Imagine you're trying to understand the meaning of the word "it" in the sentence: "The cat sat on the mat, and it purred softly." To do this, you need to figure out what "it" refers to. Your brain automatically connects "it" to "cat," even though they are separated by several words.

Self-attention allows Transformers to achieve a similar feat. It enables each word in a sequence to "look at" all other words in the sequence and determine how relevant they are to understanding its own meaning. This creates a dynamic representation of each word that takes into account its context within the entire sequence.

The Three Pillars of Self-Attention: Queries, Keys, and Values

To achieve this, self-attention relies on three key concepts:

Queries: Think of a query as a question about a word. For the word "it" in our example, the query might be "What does this pronoun refer to?"

Keys: Keys are like labels or identifiers for each word in the sequence. For "cat," the key might be "feline animal, subject of the sentence."

Values: Values are the actual representations of the words, containing information about their meaning and role in the sentence.

The Self-Attention Process

The self-attention mechanism works in three main steps:

Calculating Attention Scores: For each word (query), the model calculates an attention score with every other word (key) in the sequence. This score reflects how relevant the key is to the query. The higher the score, the more attention the query pays to that key.

Normalizing Attention Scores: These scores are then normalized using a softmax function, creating a probability distribution over the words in the sequence.

Weighted Sum: Finally, the model creates a weighted sum of the values of all words, where the weights are the normalized attention scores. This weighted sum becomes the new representation of the query word, enriched with contextual information from other relevant words.

The Beauty of Self-Attention

This mechanism allows Transformers to:

Capture long-range dependencies: Words can "attend" to each other regardless of their distance in the sequence, overcoming the limitations of RNNs.

Process information in parallel: Unlike RNNs, which process words sequentially, self-attention allows for parallel processing, significantly speeding up computation.

Learn complex relationships: By attending to different words with varying degrees of importance, Transformers can capture intricate relationships and nuances in language.

Self-attention is the key innovation that sets Transformers apart from previous architectures. It enables these models to achieve state-of-the-art performance on a wide range of NLP tasks and has paved the way for the development of powerful LLMs that are transforming the field of AI.

Chapter 4

Training Large Language Models

4.1 Data Acquisition and Preparation: Building Massive Datasets

We've explored the architecture and mechanisms that power LLMs, but these sophisticated models are only as good as the data they are trained on. Building a high-performing LLM requires a massive and diverse dataset that reflects the nuances and complexities of human language. This section delves into the crucial process of data acquisition and preparation.

The Data Hunger of LLMs

LLMs are data-hungry beasts. They thrive on vast quantities of text data to learn patterns, grammar, and semantic relationships. The larger and more diverse the dataset, the better the model's ability to understand and generate human-like text.

Think of it like learning a new language. The more books you read, conversations you have, and movies you watch, the richer your understanding of the language becomes. Similarly, LLMs require exposure to a wide range of text to grasp the intricacies of human communication.

Sources of Data

Where does this massive amount of data come from? Here are some common sources:

Web scraping: Extracting text data from websites, blogs, and online forums.

Books and articles: Utilizing digitized books, research papers, and news articles.

Code repositories: Leveraging code from platforms like GitHub to train LLMs for code generation tasks.

Social media: Analyzing social media posts, comments, and conversations.

Publicly available datasets: Utilizing curated datasets like Common Crawl, Wikipedia, and Project Gutenberg.

Data Preparation: Cleaning and Preprocessing

Once the data is acquired, it needs to be cleaned and preprocessed before it can be fed to an LLM. This involves several crucial steps:

Data cleaning: Removing irrelevant information, such as HTML tags, scripts, and markup.

Deduplication: Identifying and removing duplicate entries to ensure data quality.

Filtering: Filtering out noisy or irrelevant data, such as spam, irrelevant content, or offensive language.

Formatting: Converting the data into a consistent format that can be processed by the LLM.

Tokenization and encoding: Breaking down the text into tokens and representing them as numerical vectors, as discussed in Chapter 2.

Building a Diverse and Representative Dataset

It's not just about the quantity of data; quality and diversity are equally important. A good dataset should:

Be representative: Reflect the diversity of human language, including different writing styles, genres, and dialects.

Be balanced: Avoid over-representation of certain topics or viewpoints.

Be high-quality: Contain well-written and grammatically correct text.

Ethical Considerations

Data acquisition and preparation raise important ethical considerations:

Privacy: Ensure data is collected and used responsibly, respecting user privacy and data protection regulations.

Bias: Be mindful of potential biases in the data and take steps to mitigate them.

Attribution: Give credit to the creators of the data when possible.

By carefully curating and preparing a massive and diverse dataset, we lay the foundation for training powerful LLMs that can understand and generate human-like text with remarkable accuracy and fluency.

4.2 Optimization Algorithms: Fine-tuning for Optimal Performance

We've gathered our massive dataset, cleaned it, and preprocessed it. Now it's time to unleash the learning power of our LLM. But how exactly do these models learn from data? This is where **optimization algorithms** come into play.

Think of an LLM as a vast network of interconnected nodes, each with adjustable parameters. These parameters determine how the model processes information and generates output. The goal of training is to find the optimal values for these parameters, the values that enable the model to accurately predict the next word in a sequence, generate coherent text, and perform other language-related tasks.

The Role of Optimization Algorithms

Optimization algorithms are the engines that drive this learning process. They guide the adjustment of the model's parameters, nudging them towards optimal values that minimize errors and improve performance.

Imagine you're trying to climb a mountain. You don't know the exact path to the summit, but you can see the general direction. Optimization algorithms act like your compass and guide, helping you navigate the complex terrain of the model's parameter space and reach the peak of optimal performance.

Gradient Descent: A Fundamental Approach

One of the most fundamental optimization algorithms is **gradient descent**. It works by calculating the gradient of the model's error with respect to its parameters. The gradient indicates the direction of the steepest ascent in the error function. By moving the parameters in the opposite direction of the gradient, we can reduce the error and improve the model's performance.

Variants of Gradient Descent

There are several variants of gradient descent, each with its own strengths and weaknesses:

Stochastic Gradient Descent (SGD): This variant updates the parameters based on the error calculated from a small batch of data, making it faster and more efficient than standard gradient descent.

Adam: This popular algorithm combines the benefits of two other optimization methods, momentum and RMSprop, to achieve faster and more stable convergence.

Adagrad: This algorithm adapts the learning rate for each parameter, making it well-suited for sparse data.

Fine-tuning: Adapting to Specific Tasks

While pre-training on a massive dataset provides a strong foundation, LLMs often require fine-tuning to achieve optimal performance on specific tasks. Fine-tuning involves further training the model on a smaller, task-specific dataset. This allows the model to adapt its parameters and learn the nuances of the target task.

For example, if we want to use an LLM for machine translation, we might fine-tune it on a dataset of parallel sentences in the source and target languages. This would help the model learn the specific patterns and vocabulary relevant to translation.

Hyperparameter Tuning: Finding the Sweet Spot

Optimization algorithms have their own set of parameters, called **hyperparameters**. These hyperparameters control the learning process itself, such as the learning rate, batch size, and momentum. Finding the optimal values for these hyperparameters is crucial for achieving the best performance.

This process, known as **hyperparameter tuning**, often involves trial and error, experimenting with different values and evaluating the model's performance on a validation set.

By carefully selecting the right optimization algorithm and fine-tuning the model with appropriate hyperparameters, we can unlock the full potential of LLMs and achieve remarkable results in various language-related tasks.

4.3 Hardware and Infrastructure: The Computational Demands of LLMs

Training and deploying large language models is no small feat. These complex models, with their billions of parameters and massive datasets, require significant computational resources.[1] This section explores the hardware and infrastructure necessary to support the demanding world of LLMs.

The Need for Speed: GPUs and TPUs

Traditional CPUs, while versatile, are not optimized for the parallel computations required by deep learning models.[2] This is where specialized hardware accelerators come in:

GPUs (Graphics Processing Units): Originally designed for rendering graphics, GPUs excel at parallel processing, making them ideal for the matrix operations that underpin deep learning.[3]

TPUs (Tensor Processing Units): Developed specifically for machine learning, TPUs offer even greater performance and efficiency for deep learning tasks compared to GPUs.[4]

These accelerators significantly speed up the training process, reducing the time it takes to train an LLM from weeks or months to days or even hours.[5]

Memory Matters: High-Bandwidth Memory

LLMs also require vast amounts of memory to store the model parameters, activations, and training data.[6] High-bandwidth memory is crucial for efficient data access and transfer, preventing bottlenecks that can slow down the training process.[7]

Distributed Training: Scaling Across Multiple Devices

To further accelerate training, LLMs are often trained across multiple GPUs or TPUs in a distributed manner.[8] This involves dividing the training data and model parameters across multiple devices, allowing them to work in parallel and reduce training time.[9]

The Cloud: A Scalable Solution

Cloud computing platforms, such as Google Cloud, AWS, and Azure, provide scalable and cost-effective solutions for training and deploying LLMs.[10] These platforms offer access to powerful hardware, including GPUs and TPUs, as well as managed services that simplify the infrastructure management.[11]

Beyond Training: Inference and Deployment

Even after training, LLMs require significant computational resources for inference, the process of generating output from the model.[12] This can be challenging for resource-constrained devices, such as mobile phones or embedded systems.

Techniques like model optimization and compression can help reduce the size and computational demands of LLMs, making them more suitable for deployment on a wider range of devices.[13]

Energy Consumption: An Environmental Concern

The computational demands of LLMs translate to significant energy consumption.[14] This raises concerns about the environmental impact of training and deploying these models. Researchers are actively exploring ways to improve the energy efficiency of LLMs and reduce their carbon footprint.[15]

The Future of LLM Hardware and Infrastructure

The field of LLM hardware and infrastructure is constantly evolving, with new and more powerful accelerators being developed. As LLMs continue to grow in size and complexity, the demand for specialized hardware and scalable infrastructure will only increase.

By understanding the computational demands of LLMs and investing in the right hardware and infrastructure, we can unlock the full potential of these powerful models and drive innovation in various fields.

Chapter 5

Prompt Engineering and Fine-tuning

5.1 Crafting Effective Prompts: Guiding LLM Outputs

Imagine having a powerful tool at your disposal, capable of generating creative text formats, translating languages, and answering your questions in a comprehensive and informative way. That's the potential of LLMs. But to truly unlock their power, you need to know how to communicate effectively with them. This is where **prompt engineering** comes in.

Prompt engineering is the art and science of crafting effective prompts – the input you provide to an LLM – to guide its output and achieve desired results. It's like giving clear and specific instructions to a talented chef, ensuring they create the culinary masterpiece you envision.

The Importance of Clear and Specific Prompts

LLMs are incredibly powerful, but they're not mind readers. They rely on your prompts to understand what you want them to do. A vague or ambiguous prompt can lead to unexpected or irrelevant outputs. On the other hand, a well-crafted prompt can guide the LLM towards generating exactly what you need.

Think of it like asking for directions. If you simply say, "I want to go somewhere interesting," you might end up anywhere. But if you say, "I'm looking for a historical museum with interactive exhibits within a 10-mile radius," you're much more likely to get the directions you need.

Key Principles of Effective Prompt Engineering

Here are some key principles to keep in mind when crafting prompts:

Be clear and concise: Use precise language and avoid ambiguity. Clearly state what you want the LLM to do.

Provide context: Give the LLM the necessary background information to understand your request.

Specify the desired output: Tell the LLM what kind of output you're looking for (e.g., a summary, a poem, a code snippet).

Use examples: Provide examples of the desired output to help the LLM understand your expectations.

Experiment and iterate: Don't be afraid to try different prompts and refine them based on the LLM's responses.

Types of Prompts

There are various types of prompts you can use, depending on your goal:

Instructional prompts: Tell the LLM what to do (e.g., "Write a short story about a cat who goes on an adventure").

Completion prompts: Provide the beginning of a text and ask the LLM to complete it (e.g., "The old house stood on a hill overlooking the sea...").

Question-answering prompts: Ask the LLM a question (e.g., "What is the capital of France?").

Dialogue prompts: Engage the LLM in a conversation (e.g., "Let's discuss the pros and cons of renewable energy").

Advanced Prompt Engineering Techniques

As you become more proficient in prompt engineering, you can explore advanced techniques, such as:

Chain-of-thought prompting: Guide the LLM through a reasoning process by providing intermediate steps.

Few-shot learning: Provide a few examples of the desired output to help the LLM generalize to new inputs.

Prompt engineering with tools: Utilize external tools, such as search engines or calculators, to enhance the LLM's capabilities.

By mastering the art of prompt engineering, you can unlock the full potential of LLMs and harness their power to generate creative text formats, translate languages, write different kinds of creative content, and answer your questions in[1] a comprehensive and informative[2] way.

5.2 Fine-tuning for Specific Tasks: Adapting LLMs to Your Needs

While pre-training LLMs on massive datasets equips them with a broad understanding of language, they often need further refinement to excel at specific tasks. This is where **fine-tuning** comes in. Think of it as taking a talented all-around athlete and providing them with specialized coaching to become a champion in a particular sport.

Fine-tuning involves taking a pre-trained LLM and training it further on a smaller, more focused dataset that is specific to the task you want it to perform. This process allows the model to adapt its knowledge and parameters to better suit the nuances and requirements of the target task.

Why Fine-tune?

Fine-tuning offers several benefits:

Improved performance: By tailoring the model to a specific task, you can significantly boost its accuracy and effectiveness.

Reduced training time: Fine-tuning requires less time and resources compared to training a model from scratch.

Enhanced generalization: Fine-tuning can help the model generalize better to new, unseen data within the target domain.

Domain adaptation: You can adapt a general-purpose LLM to a specific domain, such as medical, legal, or financial, by fine-tuning it on domain-specific data.

How to Fine-tune an LLM

The fine-tuning process typically involves the following steps:

1 Choose a pre-trained LLM: Select a model that is suitable for your task and has been pre-trained on a large and diverse dataset.

2 Gather a task-specific dataset: Collect or create a dataset that is relevant to your target task and contains examples of the desired input-output pairs.

3 Prepare the data: Clean, preprocess, and format the data to make it compatible with the LLM.

4 Fine-tune the model: Train the pre-trained LLM on the task-specific dataset, adjusting its parameters to optimize performance on the target task.

5 Evaluate the model: Assess the model's performance on a held-out test set to ensure it generalizes well to new data.

Fine-tuning Techniques

There are various techniques for fine-tuning LLMs:

Task-specific fine-tuning: This involves fine-tuning the model on a dataset that is specifically designed for the target task, such as sentiment analysis, question answering, or text summarization.

Domain-specific fine-tuning: This involves fine-tuning the model on a dataset that is representative of a specific domain, such as medical or legal text, to improve its understanding of domain-specific language and concepts.

Multi-task fine-tuning: This involves fine-tuning the model on multiple tasks simultaneously, allowing it to learn more generalizable representations.

Choosing the Right Approach

The best approach for fine-tuning depends on your specific needs and the available resources. Consider factors such as the size and quality of your dataset, the complexity of the task, and the computational resources at your disposal.

By carefully fine-tuning LLMs, you can adapt these powerful models to your specific needs and unlock their full potential for a wide range of applications.

5.3 Prompt Engineering Techniques: Advanced Strategies for Control

As we delve deeper into the world of prompt engineering, we uncover a treasure trove of advanced techniques that allow for even greater control and precision in guiding LLM outputs. These techniques leverage the nuances of language and the intricacies of LLMs to elicit more accurate, relevant, and creative responses.

1. Chain-of-Thought Prompting: Guiding Reasoning

LLMs can sometimes struggle with complex reasoning tasks that require multiple steps. **Chain-of-thought prompting** helps overcome this by explicitly guiding the LLM through a step-by-step reasoning process.

Instead of just asking for the answer, you provide a series of intermediate reasoning steps, demonstrating how to arrive at the solution. This encourages the LLM to follow a similar thought process, improving its ability to solve complex problems.

Example:

Standard Prompt: "Roger has 5 tennis balls. He buys 2 more cans of tennis balls. Each can has 3 tennis balls. How many tennis balls does he have now?"

Chain-of-Thought[1] Prompt: "Roger has 5 tennis balls. He buys 2 more cans of tennis balls. Each can has 3 tennis balls. How many tennis balls does he have now?[2] Let's think step by step. First, calculate the total number of balls from the cans: 2 cans * 3 balls/can = 6 balls. Then, add that to the initial number of balls: 6 balls + 5 balls = 11 balls. So the answer is 11."

2. Few-Shot Learning: Learning from Examples

LLMs are remarkably adept at learning from examples. **Few-shot learning** leverages this capability by providing the model with a few examples of the desired input-output pairs before presenting the actual prompt.

This allows the LLM to quickly grasp the underlying pattern or task and generate more accurate and relevant responses, even with limited training data.

Example:

Prompt: "Translate the following sentence into Spanish: The cat sat on the mat."

Few-Shot Prompt:

"English: The dog barked. Spanish: El perro ladró."

"English: The bird flew. Spanish: El pájaro voló."

"Translate the following sentence into Spanish: The cat sat on the mat."

3. Prompt Engineering with Tools: Expanding Capabilities

LLMs can be further enhanced by integrating them with external tools, such as search engines, calculators, or databases. This allows them to access and process information beyond their internal knowledge, expanding their capabilities and enabling them to perform more complex tasks.

For example, you could use a prompt that instructs the LLM to search for relevant information on the web before answering a question, or to use a calculator to perform mathematical calculations.

4. Controlling Style and Tone

You can guide the LLM to generate text in a specific style or tone by providing explicit instructions or examples in the prompt.

Example:

Prompt: "Write a short story about a haunted house in the style of Edgar Allan Poe."

5. Generating Different Creative Text Formats

By providing clear instructions and examples, you can prompt LLMs to generate various creative text formats, such as poems, scripts, musical pieces, email, letters, etc.

Example:

Prompt: "Compose a sonnet about the beauty of nature."

Continuous Refinement

Prompt engineering is an iterative process. Experiment with different techniques, analyze the LLM's responses, and refine your prompts to achieve the desired level of control and precision. The more you practice, the better you'll become at guiding LLMs to generate high-quality outputs that meet your specific needs.

Chapter 6

Evaluating LLM Performance

6.1 Metrics for Language Generation: Assessing Fluency and Coherence

Building a large language model is one thing, but how do we know if it's actually any good? Evaluating the performance of LLMs is crucial to understand their strengths and weaknesses, track progress, and guide further development. This involves using a variety of metrics to assess different aspects of their generated output, with a particular focus on fluency and coherence.

Fluency: Does it Sound Natural?

Fluency refers to how natural and grammatically correct the generated text sounds. A fluent LLM produces text that flows smoothly, follows grammatical rules, and uses appropriate vocabulary. Here are some common metrics to assess fluency:

Perplexity: This metric measures how well the LLM predicts the next word in a sequence. Lower perplexity scores indicate better fluency, as the model is more confident in its predictions.

Grammaticality: Automated tools and human evaluation can be used to assess the grammatical correctness of the generated text.

Readability: Metrics like the Flesch-Kincaid readability score can assess how easy the text is to read and understand.

Coherence: Does it Make Sense?

Coherence refers to how well the generated text hangs together logically. A coherent LLM produces text that is organized, consistent, and easy to follow. Here are some ways to assess coherence:

Semantic Similarity: This measures how closely related the meanings of consecutive sentences are. Tools like cosine similarity between sentence embeddings can be used.

Topic Coherence: This evaluates whether the generated text stays on topic and avoids abrupt shifts in subject matter.

Logical Flow: Human evaluation is often crucial to assess whether the text follows a logical progression of ideas and avoids contradictions.

Beyond Fluency and Coherence

While fluency and coherence are essential, evaluating LLMs also involves considering other factors, such as:

Relevance: Does the generated text address the prompt or question appropriately?

Factuality: Is the information presented accurate and truthful?

Originality: Does the LLM generate novel and creative text, or does it simply regurgitate information from the training data?

Bias and Fairness: Does the generated text exhibit any biases or perpetuate harmful stereotypes?

Challenges in Evaluation

Evaluating LLMs presents unique challenges:

Subjectivity: Human language is inherently subjective, and what constitutes "good" language can vary depending on the context and individual preferences.

Lack of Ground Truth: For many tasks, there is no single "correct" answer, making it difficult to define objective evaluation criteria.

Evolving Capabilities: LLMs are constantly evolving, and new metrics and evaluation methods need to be developed to keep pace with their advancements.

The Importance of Human Evaluation

While automated metrics can provide valuable insights, human evaluation remains crucial for assessing the overall quality and effectiveness of LLMs. Humans can judge aspects like coherence, relevance, and originality that are difficult to capture with automated metrics alone.

By combining automated metrics with human evaluation, we can gain a comprehensive understanding of LLM performance and guide their development towards generating truly human-like language.

6.2 Benchmark Datasets and Evaluation Frameworks

Evaluating LLMs effectively requires standardized benchmarks that allow for fair and consistent comparisons across different models.[1] These benchmarks typically consist of datasets and evaluation frameworks designed to assess specific capabilities and identify areas for improvement.[2]

Benchmark Datasets: The Testing Grounds

Benchmark datasets are curated collections of examples that challenge LLMs with various tasks and measure their performance.[3] These datasets cover a wide range of language-based tasks, such as:

Question answering: Datasets like SQuAD (Stanford Question Answering Dataset) and Natural Questions evaluate the LLM's ability to answer questions based on given text.[4]

Text summarization: Datasets like CNN/Daily Mail and XSum assess the LLM's ability to condense lengthy articles into concise summaries.[5]

Natural language inference: Datasets like SNLI (Stanford Natural Language Inference) and MultiNLI test the LLM's ability to understand the relationship between two sentences (e.g., entailment, contradiction, neutral).[6]

Sentiment analysis: Datasets like IMDB and SST (Stanford Sentiment Treebank) evaluate the LLM's ability to identify the sentiment expressed in a piece of text (e.g., positive, negative, neutral).[7]

Machine translation: Datasets like WMT (Workshop on Machine Translation) assess the LLM's ability to translate text between different languages.

Evaluation Frameworks: Standardized Metrics and Tools

Evaluation frameworks provide standardized metrics and tools for assessing LLM performance on benchmark datasets.[8] These frameworks often include:

Automatic metrics: These are quantitative measures that can be computed automatically, such as accuracy, precision, recall, F1-score, BLEU (for machine translation), and ROUGE (for text summarization).[9]

Human evaluation: This involves human judges assessing the quality of LLM outputs, often using rating scales or comparative judgments.[10]

Leaderboards: These platforms track the performance of different LLMs on benchmark datasets, providing a way to compare and rank models.[11]

Examples of Benchmark Datasets and Frameworks:

GLUE (General Language Understanding Evaluation): A collection of nine diverse natural language understanding tasks, along with a leaderboard for comparing model performance.[12]

SuperGLUE: A more challenging successor to GLUE, with tasks that require more complex reasoning and common sense.[13]

HELM (Holistic Evaluation of Language Models): A comprehensive evaluation framework developed by Stanford University, covering a wide range of metrics and tasks.[14]

EleutherAI Eval: A suite of over 200 tasks designed to evaluate the capabilities of LLMs across various domains.[15]

Why Benchmarks Matter

Benchmark datasets and evaluation frameworks are essential for:

Tracking progress: They provide a way to measure the progress of LLMs over time and identify areas where further research is needed.[16]

Comparing models: They enable fair and consistent comparisons between different LLMs, helping researchers and developers choose the best model for their needs.[17]

Driving innovation: They encourage the development of new and improved LLMs by providing clear goals and evaluation criteria.

By utilizing standardized benchmarks and evaluation frameworks, we can ensure that LLMs are evaluated rigorously and objectively, driving progress in the field and fostering the development of more capable and reliable language models.[18]

6.3 Human Evaluation: The Importance of Qualitative Assessment

While we can measure many aspects of LLM output with automated metrics, the nuances of human language often require a more subjective and nuanced approach.[1] This is where **human evaluation** becomes crucial. It brings in the human perspective, capturing qualities that are difficult to quantify with algorithms alone.[2]

Why Human Evaluation Matters

Here's why human input is essential in assessing LLMs:

Capturing Subjectivity: Language is inherently subjective.[3] What sounds natural, engaging, or informative can vary depending on individual preferences, cultural backgrounds, and specific contexts. Human evaluators can capture these nuances, providing a more holistic assessment of the LLM's output.[4]

Assessing Coherence and Meaning: While metrics like semantic similarity can measure the relatedness of sentences, they may not fully capture the overall coherence and meaning of a text. Human evaluators can judge whether the text flows logically, makes sense as a whole, and conveys a clear message.

Evaluating Creativity and Originality: Determining whether an LLM generates truly original and creative text is a complex task. Human evaluators can assess the novelty of ideas, the use of stylistic devices, and the overall creativity of the output.[5]

Identifying Biases and Ethical Concerns: LLMs can sometimes generate biased or harmful outputs, reflecting biases present in the training data.[6] Human evaluators can identify these issues, ensuring that the LLM's output aligns with ethical guidelines and societal values.[7]

Methods of Human Evaluation

There are various methods for conducting human evaluation:

Rating scales: Evaluators assign scores to different aspects of the LLM output, such as fluency, coherence, relevance, and originality.[8]

Comparative judgments: Evaluators compare the output of different LLMs or different versions of the same LLM, choosing the one they prefer or deem to be of higher quality.

Qualitative feedback: Evaluators provide detailed feedback on the LLM output, explaining their judgments and highlighting specific strengths and weaknesses.[9]

Challenges of Human Evaluation

Human evaluation also comes with its own set of challenges:

Subjectivity: Different evaluators may have different opinions and preferences, leading to variability in judgments.[10]

Cost and Time: Human evaluation can be time-consuming and expensive, especially for large-scale evaluations.[11]

Cognitive Biases: Evaluators may be influenced by their own biases and expectations, affecting their judgments.[12]

Best Practices for Human Evaluation

To ensure reliable and meaningful results, it's important to follow best practices for human evaluation:

Clear guidelines: Provide evaluators with clear and specific guidelines on what to assess and how to provide feedback.[13]

Diverse pool of evaluators: Include evaluators from diverse backgrounds and with different perspectives to reduce bias.[14]

Calibration and training: Calibrate evaluators to ensure consistency in their judgments and provide training on the specific task and evaluation criteria.[15]

Statistical analysis: Use appropriate statistical methods to analyze the human evaluation data and account for variability in judgments.

The Future of Human Evaluation

As LLMs become more sophisticated, human evaluation will continue to play a critical role in assessing their capabilities and ensuring they align with human values.[16] Researchers are exploring new methods for human evaluation, such as crowdsourcing and interactive evaluation platforms, to make the process more efficient and scalable.[17]

By combining human evaluation with automated metrics, we can gain a more comprehensive understanding of LLM performance and guide their development towards generating truly human-like language that is both fluent, coherent, and ethically sound.[18]

Chapter 7

Generative AI Beyond Text

7.1 Multimodal LLMs: Integrating Text with Images and Other Data

While we've largely focused on LLMs that process and generate text, the world around us is rich with diverse forms of data. Images, audio, video, sensor readings – these all contribute to our understanding of the world. **Multimodal LLMs** are emerging as a powerful new frontier in AI, capable of integrating and understanding information from multiple modalities, not just text.[1]

Breaking Down the Walls Between Modalities

Traditional AI models have often been confined to specific domains. Natural language processing models focused on text, computer vision models on images, and speech recognition models on audio. Multimodal LLMs break down these walls, allowing for a more holistic and integrated understanding of information.[2]

Think of it like the human brain. We seamlessly integrate information from our senses – sight, sound, touch, smell, and taste – to form a coherent understanding of our surroundings.[3] Multimodal LLMs aim to replicate this capability, enabling AI systems to perceive and interact with the world in a more human-like way.[4]

How Multimodal LLMs Work

Multimodal LLMs combine different types of data into a shared representation space.[5] This allows the model to learn relationships and connections between different modalities.[6] For example, a multimodal LLM might learn that the word "cat" is associated with images of cats, the sound of a cat meowing, and even the tactile sensation of petting a cat.

This integration is achieved through various techniques:

Joint embedding architectures: These architectures learn to map different modalities into a shared embedding space, where similar concepts across modalities are represented by nearby vectors.[7]

Cross-attention mechanisms: These mechanisms allow the model to attend to information from different modalities when processing a specific modality, capturing cross-modal relationships.[8]

Transformer-based architectures: The Transformer architecture, with its ability to handle sequential data and capture long-range dependencies, has proven to be highly effective for multimodal learning.[9]

Applications of Multimodal LLMs

The ability to integrate information from multiple modalities opens up a world of possibilities:

Image captioning: Generating descriptive captions for images, combining visual understanding with language generation.[10]

Visual question answering: Answering questions about images, requiring the model to understand both the visual content and the natural language question.[11]

Text-to-image generation: Creating images from textual descriptions, bridging the gap between language and visual representation.[12]

Audio-visual speech recognition: Improving speech recognition by incorporating visual information from lip movements.[13]

Multimodal dialogue systems: Building chatbots that can understand and respond to both text and images, enabling more natural and engaging conversations.[14]

Examples of Multimodal LLMs

CLIP (Contrastive Language-Image Pre-training): Developed by OpenAI, CLIP learns to associate images and text through contrastive learning, enabling zero-shot image classification and other multimodal tasks.[15]

DALL-E 2: Also from OpenAI, DALL-E 2 can generate realistic and creative images from textual descriptions, demonstrating the power of multimodal LLMs for creative applications.[16]

Flamingo: Developed by DeepMind, Flamingo is a visual language model that can perform various tasks, including visual question answering, image captioning, and multiple-choice visual question answering.[17]

The Future of Multimodal LLMs

Multimodal LLMs represent a significant step towards more general-purpose AI systems that can understand and interact with the world in a more human-like way. As these models continue to evolve, we can expect to see even more innovative applications that bridge the gap between different modalities and unlock new possibilities in fields like robotics, healthcare, and education.

7.2 Applications in Image Generation and Code Synthesis

Multimodal LLMs are pushing the boundaries of generative AI, enabling exciting new applications that go beyond text. Two areas where these models are making a significant impact are:

1. Image Generation: From Text to Pixels

Imagine describing a scene in words and having an AI model generate a photorealistic image that perfectly captures your description. This is the power of multimodal LLMs in image generation.

These models learn to associate textual descriptions with visual representations, allowing them to create images from scratch based on textual prompts. This has a wide range of applications:

Creative arts: Artists and designers can use these models to explore new ideas, generate inspiration, and create novel visual content.

Content creation: Marketing teams, advertisers, and content creators can generate images for websites, social media, and other platforms, tailored to specific needs and themes.

E-commerce: Generate product images from textual descriptions, saving time and resources for online retailers.

Gaming: Create realistic and diverse in-game assets, such as characters, environments, and objects.

Fashion: Generate new clothing designs and visualize different styles and combinations.

Examples of Image Generation Models:

DALL-E 2 (OpenAI): Generates high-quality images from textual descriptions, capturing complex concepts and compositions.

Imagen (Google): Another powerful text-to-image model that excels at generating photorealistic images with high fidelity.

Midjourney: A popular AI art generator that creates stunning visuals based on user prompts, often with a surreal or artistic style.

Stable Diffusion: An open-source text-to-image model known for its flexibility and ability to generate diverse images.

2. Code Synthesis: From Natural Language to Code

Multimodal LLMs are also transforming the way we write code. By integrating natural language understanding with code generation capabilities, these models can translate natural language descriptions into executable code.

This has the potential to:

Accelerate software development: Automate repetitive coding tasks, generate code snippets from natural language descriptions, and even create entire programs from scratch.

Lower the barrier to entry: Allow people with limited coding experience to express their ideas in natural language and have the AI translate them into code.

Improve code quality: Generate code that is more consistent, efficient, and less prone to errors.

Examples of Code Synthesis Models:

Codex (OpenAI): A descendant of GPT-3 fine-tuned for code generation, Codex can generate code in multiple programming languages, including Python, JavaScript, and C++.

AlphaCode (DeepMind): This model can solve competitive programming problems, demonstrating its ability to understand complex logic and generate efficient code.

GitHub Copilot: A code completion tool powered by Codex, Copilot provides suggestions and auto-completes code as you type, improving developer productivity.

Challenges and Ethical Considerations

While the applications of multimodal LLMs in image generation and code synthesis are vast and exciting, they also raise important challenges and ethical considerations:

Bias and fairness: These models can inherit biases from the training data, leading to the generation of images or code that perpetuate harmful stereotypes or discriminate against certain groups.

Misinformation and manipulation: The ability to generate realistic images and convincing code could be misused for creating fake content or spreading misinformation.

Intellectual property: Questions arise about the ownership and copyright of images and code generated by AI models.

It's crucial to address these challenges and develop these technologies responsibly, ensuring that they are used for beneficial purposes and do not exacerbate existing societal issues.

By carefully considering the ethical implications and addressing the potential risks, we can harness the power of multimodal LLMs to unlock new creative possibilities and drive innovation in various fields.

7.3 The Future of Generative AI: Expanding Creative Possibilities

Generative AI is still in its early stages, yet it's already transforming how we create and interact with the world. As this technology continues to evolve, we can expect even more exciting possibilities to emerge, pushing the boundaries of creativity and innovation.[1]

Here are some key trends and predictions for the future of generative AI:

1. Towards More General-Purpose AI

Current generative models often excel in specific domains, like text or image generation.[2] The future lies in developing more general-purpose AI that can seamlessly integrate and generate information across multiple modalities. Imagine an AI that can understand and respond to your requests in natural language, generate images and videos based on your descriptions, and even compose music that matches your mood.

2. Enhanced Human-AI Collaboration[3]

Generative AI is not meant to replace human creativity but to augment it.[4] We can expect more sophisticated tools and interfaces that empower artists, writers, musicians, and designers to collaborate with AI, leveraging its strengths while retaining human control and artistic vision.[5]

3. Personalized and Interactive Experiences

Generative AI will enable the creation of highly personalized and interactive experiences.[6] Imagine video games where the storylines and characters adapt to your choices, educational materials that tailor themselves to your learning style, or virtual worlds that respond to your imagination in real-time.[7]

4. Democratization of Creativity

Generative AI has the potential to democratize access to creative tools and empower anyone to express their ideas, regardless of their technical skills.[8] This could lead to a surge in user-generated content and a more diverse and inclusive creative landscape.

5. New Forms of Art and Expression

Generative AI is already pushing the boundaries of art and expression, with new forms like AI-generated music, poetry, and visual art emerging.[9] As these models become more sophisticated, we can expect even more innovative and thought-provoking creations that challenge our understanding of creativity and art.[10]

6. Ethical and Responsible Development

As generative AI becomes more powerful, it's crucial to address the ethical implications and ensure responsible development.[11] This includes mitigating biases, preventing misuse, and ensuring transparency and accountability in the use of these technologies.[12]

7. Applications Across Industries

The applications of generative AI extend far beyond the creative industries. We can expect to see these models being used in healthcare for drug discovery and personalized medicine, in engineering for design optimization and material discovery, and in science for generating new hypotheses and accelerating research.

Challenges and Opportunities

The future of generative AI is filled with both challenges and opportunities. We need to address issues like bias, misinformation, and the potential for job displacement while also harnessing the power of these technologies to solve pressing problems and create a more equitable and fulfilling future.

By fostering collaboration between researchers, developers, artists, and policymakers, we can ensure that generative AI is developed and used in a way that benefits humanity and unlocks new creative possibilities.

Chapter 8

Ethical Considerations and Responsible AI

8.1 Bias in LLMs: Identifying and Mitigating Unfair Outputs

Large language models are trained on massive amounts of data, reflecting the world's information – both good and bad.[1] This means they can inadvertently learn and perpetuate biases present in the data, leading to unfair or discriminatory outputs.[2] Addressing bias in LLMs is crucial for building responsible and ethical AI systems.[3]

How Bias Manifests in LLMs

Bias can appear in various forms:

Gender bias: Associating certain professions or roles with specific genders (e.g., "nurse" with female, "engineer" with male).[4]

Racial bias: Using stereotypes or making harmful generalizations about certain racial or ethnic groups.[5]

Religious bias: Expressing prejudice or discriminatory views towards certain religions or beliefs.[6]

Cultural bias: Favoring or devaluing certain cultural practices or perspectives.[7]

Socioeconomic bias: Making assumptions or judgments based on socioeconomic status.[8]

Sources of Bias

Bias in LLMs can stem from various sources:

Training data: If the training data contains biased information or underrepresents certain groups, the model will likely learn and perpetuate those biases.[9]

Model architecture: The design choices of the model itself can introduce or amplify biases.[10]

Training process: The optimization algorithms and hyperparameters used during training can influence the model's susceptibility to bias.[11]

Human feedback: If human feedback used during training or fine-tuning is biased, it can reinforce biases in the model.

Identifying Bias

Detecting bias in LLMs requires careful analysis and evaluation:

Quantitative analysis: Analyzing the model's output for statistically significant differences in how it treats different groups or concepts.[12]

Qualitative analysis: Examining the model's output for subtle biases, stereotypes, or discriminatory language.[13]

Human evaluation: Engaging human evaluators to assess the fairness and inclusivity of the model's output.

Benchmark datasets: Using benchmark datasets specifically designed to evaluate bias in LLMs.[14]

Mitigating Bias

Addressing bias in LLMs is an ongoing challenge, but there are several strategies to mitigate its effects:

Data curation: Carefully curate the training data to ensure diversity and representation, and remove or re-weight biased examples.[15]

Data augmentation: Generate synthetic data to balance the representation of different groups or perspectives.[16]

Bias detection and correction: Develop techniques to automatically detect and correct biases in the model's output.[17]

Adversarial training: Train the model to be robust to adversarial examples that exploit biases.[18]

Fairness constraints: Incorporate fairness constraints into the model's objective function during training.[19]

Human oversight: Involve human experts in the training and evaluation process to identify and address potential biases.[20]

The Importance of Ongoing Efforts

Mitigating bias in LLMs is an ongoing process that requires continuous effort and vigilance. As LLMs become more powerful and pervasive, it's crucial to prioritize fairness, inclusivity, and ethical considerations in their development and deployment.

By actively addressing bias, we can ensure that LLMs are used to promote a more just and equitable society, where everyone has equal access to opportunities and resources.

8.2 Misinformation and Malicious Use: Addressing Potential Harms

While LLMs offer incredible potential for good, they can also be exploited for malicious purposes or unintentionally contribute to the spread of misinformation. Addressing these potential harms is crucial for ensuring responsible development and deployment of this powerful technology.

The Misinformation Threat

LLMs can generate highly convincing and coherent text, making them susceptible to misuse for generating fake news, propaganda, or other forms of misinformation. This can have serious consequences, eroding trust in information sources, manipulating public opinion, and even inciting violence.

Malicious Use Cases

Beyond misinformation, LLMs can be exploited for various malicious purposes:

Generating spam and phishing content: Creating large volumes of spam emails or social media posts, or crafting convincing phishing messages to trick people into revealing sensitive information.

Impersonating individuals: Generating text that mimics the writing style of real people, potentially for fraud, identity theft, or social engineering.

Creating deepfakes: Generating realistic but fabricated audio or video content, potentially for defamation, political manipulation, or spreading false narratives.

Automating malicious attacks: Using LLMs to generate malicious code, automate social engineering attacks, or create sophisticated botnets.

Addressing the Harms

Mitigating the risks of misinformation and malicious use requires a multi-faceted approach:

1. Technical Measures:

Developing detection mechanisms: Building tools and techniques to identify AI-generated text and distinguish it from human-written content.

Watermarking and provenance tracking: Embedding watermarks or other markers in LLM-generated content to track its origin and identify potential manipulations.

Content filtering and moderation: Implementing systems to filter out harmful or misleading content generated by LLMs.

Rate limiting and access controls: Restricting access to LLMs to prevent malicious actors from abusing them.

2. Education and Awareness:

Educating the public: Raising awareness about the potential for AI-generated misinformation and providing resources to help people identify and critically evaluate information.

Training developers: Educating LLM developers about the ethical implications of their work and encouraging responsible design and deployment practices.

Promoting media literacy: Equipping people with the skills and knowledge to critically analyze information and distinguish between credible and unreliable sources.

3. Policy and Regulation:

Developing ethical guidelines: Establishing clear ethical guidelines for the development and use of LLMs, emphasizing transparency, accountability, and human oversight.

Enacting legislation: Exploring legal frameworks to address the spread of AI-generated misinformation and hold malicious actors accountable.

International cooperation: Fostering international collaboration to address the global challenges posed by LLMs and ensure responsible development and use worldwide.

4. Collaboration and Responsibility

Addressing the potential harms of LLMs requires a collaborative effort between researchers, developers, policymakers, and the public. By working together, we can harness the power of these technologies for good while mitigating the risks and ensuring a safe and beneficial future for all.

It's crucial to remember that LLMs are tools, and like any tool, they can be used for both beneficial and harmful purposes. By promoting responsible development, raising awareness, and implementing appropriate safeguards, we can minimize the risks and maximize the benefits of this transformative technology.

8.3 Building Ethical and Trustworthy Generative AI Systems

Generative AI holds immense potential, but it also presents ethical challenges that must be addressed to ensure these technologies are used responsibly and beneficially. Building ethical and trustworthy generative AI systems requires a commitment to key principles and proactive measures throughout the development and deployment lifecycle.

Key Principles for Ethical Generative AI

Beneficence: Generative AI should be developed and used for the benefit of humanity, promoting well-being, and avoiding harm.

Non-maleficence: These technologies should not be used to cause harm, deceive, or manipulate individuals or groups.

Autonomy: Generative AI should respect human autonomy and avoid undermining human agency or decision-making.

Justice: These technologies should be developed and used in a fair and equitable manner, avoiding bias and discrimination.

Explainability: The decision-making processes of generative AI systems should be transparent and understandable, enabling accountability and trust.

Privacy: Generative AI should respect individual privacy and protect sensitive data.

Accountability: Developers and deployers of generative AI should be accountable for the impacts of these technologies.

Practical Steps for Building Trustworthy Generative AI

Ethical Data Practices:

Data Collection: Ensure data is collected ethically, with informed consent and respect for privacy.

Data Curation: Carefully curate training data to ensure diversity, representation, and fairness, mitigating bias.

Data Security: Implement robust data security measures to protect sensitive information.

Responsible Design and Development:

Bias Mitigation: Integrate bias detection and mitigation techniques throughout the development process.

Explainability: Design models with explainability in mind, making their decision-making processes transparent.

Safety and Robustness: Develop models that are robust to adversarial attacks and unexpected inputs.

Transparency and Accountability:

Documentation: Provide clear and comprehensive documentation of the model's architecture, training data, and limitations.

Auditing: Conduct regular audits to assess the model's performance, identify potential biases, and ensure ethical compliance.

Human Oversight: Incorporate human oversight in critical decision-making processes to ensure accountability.

User Education and Empowerment:

Transparency with Users: Inform users when they are interacting with generative AI systems.

Education: Educate users about the capabilities and limitations of generative AI, promoting responsible use.

Control and Agency: Provide users with control over their interactions with generative AI and empower them to make informed decisions.

Continuous Monitoring and Improvement:

Feedback Mechanisms: Establish feedback mechanisms for users and stakeholders to report concerns or identify potential harms.

Monitoring and Evaluation: Continuously monitor the model's performance and impact, adapting and improving it over time.

Collaboration: Foster collaboration between researchers, developers, policymakers, and the public to address ethical challenges and ensure responsible innovation.

Building Trust is an Ongoing Process

Building ethical and trustworthy generative AI is an ongoing process that requires continuous attention and adaptation. As these technologies evolve, new ethical challenges may arise, requiring ongoing dialogue, research, and collaboration to ensure that generative AI remains a force for good in the world.

By adhering to these principles and taking proactive steps to address ethical concerns, we can build generative AI systems that are not only powerful but also responsible, trustworthy, and beneficial to humanity.

Chapter 9

Deploying and Scaling LLMs

9.1 Model Optimization and Compression: Reducing Resource Requirements

Large language models, with their billions of parameters, can be computationally expensive to run, especially for resource-constrained environments like mobile devices or embedded systems. **Model optimization and compression** techniques aim to reduce the size and computational demands of these models without significantly sacrificing performance. This enables wider accessibility and efficient deployment across various platforms.

Why Optimize and Compress?

Reduced inference latency: Smaller models require less time to process input and generate output, leading to faster response times.

Lower memory footprint: Compressed models consume less memory, allowing them to run on devices with limited memory capacity.

Reduced storage requirements: Smaller models take up less storage space, making it easier to deploy and distribute them.

Energy efficiency: Optimized models consume less energy, contributing to environmental sustainability and reducing operational costs.

Model Optimization Techniques

Pruning: Removing unnecessary connections or parameters in the model, such as those with small weights or minimal impact on performance.

Quantization: Reducing the precision of numerical representations, such as using 8-bit integers instead of 32-bit floating-point numbers.

Knowledge distillation: Training a smaller "student" model to mimic the behavior of a larger "teacher" model, transferring knowledge and achieving comparable performance with fewer parameters.

Model Compression Techniques

Weight factorization: Decomposing weight matrices into smaller matrices, reducing the number of parameters.

Weight sharing: Sharing weights across different layers or parts of the model, reducing redundancy.

Tensor decomposition: Applying techniques like Tucker decomposition or CP decomposition to reduce the dimensionality of tensors.

Finding the Right Balance

The choice of optimization and compression techniques depends on the specific model, the target hardware, and the desired trade-off between performance and resource efficiency. It's crucial to find the right balance between reducing the model's size and maintaining its accuracy and capabilities.

Tools and Libraries

Several tools and libraries facilitate model optimization and compression:

TensorFlow Lite: A framework for deploying TensorFlow models on mobile and embedded devices, supporting various optimization techniques.

PyTorch Mobile: A toolkit for deploying PyTorch models on mobile and embedded devices, with optimization features for performance and efficiency.

OpenVINO: A toolkit for optimizing and deploying deep learning models on Intel hardware, supporting various compression and acceleration techniques.

Benefits Beyond Resource Efficiency

Model optimization and compression not only reduce resource requirements but can also improve the model's generalization ability and robustness to noisy data. By removing unnecessary parameters and focusing on the most important features, these techniques can lead to more efficient and reliable models.

Looking Ahead

As LLMs continue to grow in size and complexity, model optimization and compression will become increasingly important. Ongoing research in this area is exploring new and more effective techniques to reduce resource requirements without sacrificing performance, enabling wider accessibility and deployment of these powerful models.

9.2 Cloud Platforms and APIs: Accessing LLMs as a Service

Training and deploying large language models can be a complex and resource-intensive undertaking.[1] Fortunately, cloud platforms offer a convenient and scalable solution by providing access to LLMs as a service.[2] This allows developers and businesses to leverage the power of LLMs without the need to manage their own infrastructure or handle the complexities of model training and deployment.[3]

Benefits of Cloud-Based LLMs

Accessibility: Cloud platforms make LLMs accessible to a wider audience, including those without the resources or expertise to train and deploy their own models.

Scalability: Cloud providers offer scalable infrastructure that can handle the demands of running LLMs, allowing you to easily adjust resources as needed.[4]

Cost-effectiveness: You pay only for the resources you use, eliminating the upfront costs of hardware and maintenance associated with on-premise deployment.[5]

Ease of use: Cloud platforms provide user-friendly interfaces and APIs that simplify the process of integrating LLMs into your applications.[6]

Maintenance and updates: Cloud providers handle the maintenance and updates of the LLMs, ensuring you always have access to the latest versions and features.[7]

Major Cloud Platforms Offering LLMs

Google Cloud AI Platform: Provides access to a variety of pre-trained LLMs, including PaLM 2, and offers tools for fine-tuning and deploying models.[8]

Amazon Web Services (AWS): Offers Amazon Bedrock, a service that provides access to foundation models (FMs) from Amazon and leading AI startups, including Anthropic and Stability AI.[9]

Microsoft Azure: Provides Azure OpenAI Service, which grants access to powerful models like GPT-4, Codex, and DALL-E 2, along with tools for customization and deployment.[10]

OpenAI API: Offers API access to its models, including GPT-3, GPT-4, and others, allowing developers to integrate them into their applications.[11]

Cohere: Provides access to its language models through APIs, with a focus on natural language understanding and generation tasks.[12]

AI21 Labs: Offers access to Jurassic-1, one of the largest and most sophisticated language models, through its AI21 Studio platform.[13]

Accessing LLMs through APIs

Cloud platforms typically provide APIs (Application Programming Interfaces) that allow you to interact with LLMs programmatically.[14] These APIs enable you to:

Send prompts to the LLM: Provide input text or instructions to the model.[15]

Receive generated output: Retrieve the text, code, or other output generated by the LLM.

Customize parameters: Adjust parameters like temperature and max tokens to control the output.[16]

Fine-tune models: Fine-tune pre-trained models on your own data to improve performance on specific tasks.[17]

Choosing the Right Platform and Model

The choice of cloud platform and LLM depends on your specific needs and requirements. Consider factors such as:

Task: The specific task you want to perform (e.g., text generation, translation, question answering).

Model capabilities: The size, capabilities, and performance of the LLM.

Cost: The pricing structure and cost of using the platform and model.

Ease of integration: The ease of integrating the API into your existing systems.

Support and documentation: The level of support and documentation provided by the platform.

The Future of Cloud-Based LLMs

Cloud-based LLMs are rapidly evolving, with new models, features, and platforms emerging regularly. We can expect to see:

More specialized models: LLMs tailored to specific domains and tasks.[18]

Enhanced customization: Greater flexibility to customize and fine-tune models.

Improved accessibility: Lower costs and easier integration options.

Increased collaboration: More platforms and tools for collaboration between developers and users.

By leveraging the power of cloud platforms and APIs, developers and businesses can harness the transformative potential of LLMs to build innovative applications and solve complex problems across various industries.

9.3 Building LLM-Powered Applications: Real-World Deployment Strategies

Large language models are no longer confined to research labs. They're powering a new generation of applications that are transforming how we interact with technology and access information.[1] This section explores real-world deployment strategies for building LLM-powered applications.

1. Identify the Right Use Case

Not every problem requires an LLM. Start by identifying use cases where LLMs can truly add value. Some common applications include:

Chatbots and conversational AI: Creating more engaging and human-like conversational experiences.[2]

Content generation: Generating marketing copy, articles, summaries, and other forms of text.[3]

Code generation and assistance: Helping developers write code faster and more efficiently.[4]

Question answering and information retrieval: Providing accurate and relevant answers to user queries.[5]

Translation and summarization: Breaking down language barriers and condensing information.[6]

Personalized recommendations: Tailoring recommendations to individual user preferences.[7]

2. Choose the Right Deployment Model

Cloud-based deployment: Leverage cloud platforms and APIs to access LLMs as a service, offering scalability and ease of use.[8]

On-premise deployment: Deploy LLMs on your own infrastructure for greater control and data privacy.[9]

Edge deployment: Deploy LLMs on edge devices, such as smartphones or IoT devices, for low-latency and offline functionality.

Hybrid deployment: Combine different deployment models to optimize for specific needs and constraints.[10]

3. Design the Application Architecture

API integration: Integrate with cloud-based LLM APIs to access model functionalities.[11]

Prompt engineering: Design effective prompts to guide the LLM's output and achieve desired results.[12]

Data pipeline: Establish a pipeline for preprocessing input data and post-processing LLM output.[13]

User interface: Create a user-friendly interface for interacting with the LLM-powered application.[14]

Monitoring and feedback: Implement mechanisms to monitor the application's performance and gather user feedback.[15]

4. Ensure Scalability and Performance

Optimize the model: Use model optimization and compression techniques to reduce resource requirements.[16]

Caching: Cache frequently used responses to reduce latency and improve performance.[17]

Load balancing: Distribute traffic across multiple instances of the LLM to handle high demand.[18]

Auto-scaling: Automatically adjust resources based on usage patterns to ensure optimal performance.[19]

5. Address Ethical Considerations

Bias mitigation: Implement strategies to mitigate bias in the LLM's output.[20]

Transparency: Be transparent with users about the use of LLMs in the application.

Data privacy: Protect user data and ensure compliance with privacy regulations.[21]

Misinformation and misuse: Implement safeguards to prevent the spread of misinformation or malicious use of the LLM.[22]

Real-World Examples

Jasper.ai: An AI writing tool that uses LLMs to generate marketing copy, blog posts, and other content.[23]

GitHub Copilot: An AI code completion tool that assists developers with writing code.[24]

Duolingo: A language learning app that uses LLMs to personalize lessons and provide feedback.[25]

Replika: An AI chatbot that uses LLMs to provide companionship and emotional support.[26]

The Future of LLM-Powered Applications

LLM-powered applications are rapidly evolving, with new and innovative use cases emerging constantly. As LLMs become more capable and accessible, we can expect to see them integrated into a wider range of applications, transforming how we live, work, and interact with technology.

By following these deployment strategies and addressing ethical considerations, developers can harness the power of LLMs to create impactful and responsible applications that benefit society.

Chapter 10

The Future of LLMs and Generative AI

10.1 Emerging Trends and Research Directions

The field of large language models and generative AI is rapidly evolving, with new breakthroughs and innovations emerging constantly. This section explores some of the key trends and research directions shaping the future of this exciting field.

1. Scaling Up: Beyond Trillion-Parameter Models

While current LLMs boast impressive sizes, the trend of scaling up continues. Researchers are exploring the limits of model size, investigating the benefits and challenges of training models with trillions, or even quadrillions, of parameters. These larger models could potentially unlock new levels of understanding and generate even more sophisticated and nuanced outputs.

2. Multimodality: A Convergence of Senses

Multimodal LLMs, capable of integrating and generating information across various modalities like text, images, audio, and video, are gaining momentum. Research is focused on developing more robust and versatile multimodal models that can seamlessly bridge the gap between different forms of data, enabling applications like image captioning, text-to-image generation, and multimodal dialogue systems.

3. Reasoning and Common Sense:

While LLMs excel at pattern recognition and language generation, they often struggle with tasks that require reasoning, common sense, and understanding of the physical world. Research is ongoing to enhance LLMs with these capabilities, exploring techniques like knowledge integration, symbolic reasoning, and neuro-symbolic AI.

4. Explainability and Interpretability:

Understanding the inner workings of LLMs is crucial for building trust and ensuring responsible use. Research is focused on developing methods to explain and interpret the decision-making processes of these models, making them more transparent and accountable.

5. Efficiency and Sustainability:

Training and deploying large LLMs can be computationally expensive and energy-intensive. Research is exploring ways to improve the efficiency and sustainability of these models, including techniques like model compression, quantization, and efficient training algorithms.

6. Personalization and Adaptability:

Tailoring LLMs to individual users and specific contexts is a key research direction. This involves developing techniques for personalizing model parameters, adapting to user preferences, and learning from user interactions.

7. Human-AI Collaboration:

The future of LLMs lies in collaboration with humans, not replacement. Research is exploring ways to enhance human-AI interaction, developing tools and interfaces that empower humans to leverage the strengths of LLMs while retaining control and creativity.

8. Ethical and Societal Considerations:

As LLMs become more powerful and pervasive, addressing ethical and societal implications is crucial. Research is focused on mitigating bias, ensuring fairness, preventing misuse, and promoting responsible development and deployment.

9. Applications in Science and Engineering:

LLMs are finding applications beyond traditional language-based tasks. Research is exploring their potential in scientific discovery, drug development, material design, and other fields, where they can analyze data, generate hypotheses, and accelerate research.

10. Open-Source and Community-Driven Development:

The open-source movement is playing a crucial role in advancing LLM research and development. Open-source models, datasets, and tools are fostering collaboration, democratizing access to these technologies, and accelerating innovation.

The Road Ahead

The future of LLMs and generative AI is filled with exciting possibilities. By pushing the boundaries of research, addressing ethical considerations, and fostering collaboration, we can unlock the full potential of these technologies to benefit humanity and shape a better future.

10.2 The Impact of LLMs on Society and Industry

Large language models are no longer a futuristic concept; they're rapidly becoming a part of our everyday lives, with the potential to reshape society and industry in profound ways.[1] This section explores the multifaceted impact of LLMs, examining both the transformative potential and the challenges they present.

Transforming Industries

LLMs are poised to revolutionize various sectors:

Customer service: AI-powered chatbots and virtual assistants provide instant and personalized support, improving customer satisfaction and[2] efficiency.[3]

Content creation: LLMs assist writers, marketers, and content creators in generating high-quality content, from articles and blog posts to marketing copy and scripts.[4]

Software development: LLMs automate code generation, assist with debugging, and accelerate software development processes.[5]

Education: AI tutors provide personalized learning experiences, adapt to individual student needs, and offer immediate feedback.[6]

Healthcare: LLMs assist in medical diagnosis, drug discovery, and patient communication, improving healthcare outcomes and accessibility.[7]

Legal and finance: LLMs automate document review, contract analysis, and risk assessment, increasing efficiency and accuracy.[8]

Reshaping the Workforce

The rise of LLMs will undoubtedly impact the workforce:

Automation of tasks: LLMs can automate repetitive and mundane tasks, freeing up human workers for more creative and strategic roles.[9]

New job creation: The development and deployment of LLMs will create new jobs in fields like AI engineering, prompt engineering, and data science.[10]

Upskilling and reskilling: Workers will need to adapt and acquire new skills to thrive in an LLM-powered world.

Collaboration with AI: The future of work will likely involve humans and AI collaborating, leveraging each other's strengths.[11]

Societal Impacts

LLMs will also have broader societal implications:

Accessibility and inclusivity: LLMs can help bridge communication gaps, provide access to information for people with disabilities, and personalize learning experiences.[12]

Creativity and innovation: LLMs can empower individuals to express their creativity and generate new ideas, fostering innovation across various fields.[13]

Information access and dissemination: LLMs can help democratize access to information and facilitate knowledge sharing.[14]

Ethical considerations: The potential for bias, misinformation, and misuse requires careful consideration and responsible development.[15]

Challenges and Considerations

While the potential benefits of LLMs are immense, there are also challenges to address:

Job displacement: Automation of tasks could lead to job displacement in certain sectors, requiring proactive measures to support workers and create new opportunities.[16]

Bias and fairness: Mitigating bias in LLMs is crucial to ensure fairness and prevent discrimination.

Misinformation and manipulation: Safeguards are needed to prevent the spread of misinformation and malicious use of LLMs.[17]

Privacy and security: Protecting user data and ensuring the responsible use of LLMs are paramount.

Navigating the Future

The impact of LLMs on society and industry is a complex and evolving landscape. By embracing responsible development, fostering collaboration, and addressing ethical considerations, we can harness the transformative power of LLMs to create a more equitable, innovative, and fulfilling future for all.

10.3 The Evolving Landscape of AI-Human Collaboration

The rise of large language models is not about replacing humans but about augmenting our capabilities and creating a new era of AI-human collaboration. This evolving landscape is characterized by a shift from viewing AI as a competitor to embracing it as a partner, a tool that can enhance our creativity, productivity, and problem-solving abilities.

Complementary Strengths

The key to successful AI-human collaboration lies in recognizing the complementary strengths of each:

AI excels at:

Processing vast amounts of data

Identifying patterns and insights

Automating repetitive tasks

Generating creative content

Providing objective analysis

Humans excel at:

Critical thinking and complex reasoning

Emotional intelligence and empathy

Ethical decision-making

Contextual understanding

Creative vision and intuition

Evolving Roles and Responsibilities

As AI takes on more tasks, human roles are evolving:

From task execution to task design: Humans will focus on defining problems, setting goals, and designing tasks for AI to solve.

From manual labor to oversight and guidance: Humans will supervise AI systems, provide feedback, and ensure ethical and responsible use.

From knowledge acquisition to knowledge application: Humans will leverage AI to access and synthesize information, focusing on applying knowledge creatively and strategically.

New Forms of Collaboration

AI-human collaboration is taking on new forms:

AI as a creative partner: Artists, writers, and musicians are using AI as a tool for inspiration, exploration, and co-creation.

AI as a research assistant: Scientists and researchers are leveraging AI to analyze data, generate hypotheses, and accelerate discoveries.

AI as a personalized tutor: AI-powered educational tools provide customized learning experiences and adapt to individual needs.

AI as a decision support system: AI provides insights and recommendations to help humans make informed decisions.

Building Trust and Transparency

Successful AI-human collaboration requires trust and transparency:

Explainable AI: Understanding how AI systems make decisions is crucial for building trust and ensuring accountability.

Human-centered design: AI systems should be designed with human needs and values in mind, promoting user agency and control.

Ethical guidelines: Clear ethical guidelines are needed to ensure responsible development and use of AI in collaborative settings.

The Future of AI-Human Collaboration

The future of AI-human collaboration is filled with potential:

Enhanced productivity and creativity: AI can amplify human capabilities, leading to increased productivity and new forms of creative expression.

Solving complex problems: Humans and AI can work together to tackle complex challenges in areas like healthcare, climate change, and poverty.

Improved decision-making: AI can provide insights and analysis to support human decision-making, leading to better outcomes.

More fulfilling work: By automating mundane tasks, AI can free up humans to focus on more meaningful and engaging work.

Challenges and Opportunities

While the potential benefits are significant, there are also challenges to address:

Ensuring human control: Maintaining human oversight and preventing over-reliance on AI is crucial.

Addressing bias and fairness: AI systems should be designed to be fair and unbiased, avoiding perpetuation of harmful stereotypes.

Protecting privacy and security: Safeguarding user data and preventing misuse of AI are essential.

By navigating these challenges and embracing the opportunities, we can create a future where humans and AI work together to achieve remarkable things. The evolving landscape of AI-human collaboration holds the promise of a more innovative, productive, and fulfilling future for all.

www.ingramcontent.com/pod-product-compliance
Lightning Source LLC
LaVergne TN
LVHW012337060326
832902LV00012B/1918